BELOW
the
SURFACE

BELOW
the
SURFACE

Reflections on Life and Living

ANNE SPENCER PARRY

MARJORIE PIZER

Angus&Robertson
An imprint of HarperCollins*Publishers*

To all those people who came to us for help, without whom we could not have written this book, and in memory of Anne Spencer Parry, 1932–1985, novelist, psychotherapist and friend.

The unexamined life is not worth living

SOCRATES

Contents

Introduction

When *Below the Surface* was first published in 1982, Anne Spencer Parry and I had been psychotherapists in private practice in Sydney for twenty years. It was our attempt to extract the essence from what we had learnt about life and people in that time. For ten years we had tried to write it. We had sat and talked, made voluminous notes, written hundreds of pages but there was so much to say on so many aspects of human nature that we found it impossible to put it together in a readable form. Then suddenly, one day, Anne had an 'ah ha' moment, the idea of combining poems and short pieces of prose and, in about eight weeks, we had the first draft of the book completed. We made some copies and lent them to friends and clients for comment. We found that they read the manuscript over and over and wanted to keep it. We had to demand our copies back. We knew then that the book was ready so we found its title and published it.

Anne and I had a small publishing company called Pinchgut Press and had been publishing her novels and my poetry with some success since 1975. However, we found with *Below the Surface* that our efforts to promote it were in vain. Not a review appeared nor could we get any interest in publicising it but, to our surprise, the book sold by word of mouth. We began to receive orders from all over Australia; people rang us for copies and turned up on our doorstep to buy copies for themselves and their friends. It has sold steadily ever since. It is a most borrowed book, often borrowed and never returned.

We tried to write this book simply and with absolute clarity, for only in simplicity can the truth be tested.

We hope you experience as much joyful discovery in reading this work as we had in finding out the truths for ourselves.

Marjorie Pizer, 1993

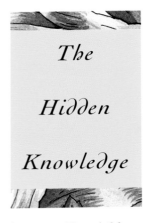

The

Hidden

Knowledge

Why do people think knowledge is hidden? For truth is as common in the world as the grains of soil in the earth or as the sands of the seas. Why do we call hidden that which is so revealed? It is because, like children, we cover our eyes with our hands and believe that we cannot be seen. We blind ourselves to avoid the truth which stands revealed in every act and every response, in every line of every face, in all the ways people live everywhere, in their buildings, the kind of work they do, the way they play, in all their institutions, both good and bad, and especially in the lies they tell. Everywhere truth stands naked in the sun and we turn away because the light hurts our eyes.

Nevertheless, because this world is a place of revealed truth, it always happens that the thing we hide from ourselves is the very thing we meet in the world. If, inside myself, I live in a prison and feel its constraints about me then, though I seek freedom wherever I go, yet will I find only prisons. For me, the hidden truth concerns imprisonment and restriction and so this is what the world will always show me. There is no way to avoid the lesson and the truth.

Simplicity is an aspect of truth;
complexity is an aspect of lies.

Do not give me a guru

Do not give me a guru
To sit at the feet of.
Do not provide me with a prophet
To follow into the wilderness.
Do not send me a seer with secrets
To guide me to life everlasting.
I am not looking any more
For someone to tell me the way.
I have found, in my life, many answers,
None of which turned out to be The Answer.
I have chosen various messiahs to
*   follow in my time,*
But each of them turned out to be false.
Now I know that I must follow my own heart
Along my own path.
Now I know that there are no answers
But only questions,
And the whole joy and anguish of living.

Healing

The task of the rescue of the soul is long
    and slow

And only those will be rescued who want to
    be rescued,

For only the soul itself can unmake

The prison it has so carefully constructed.

How delicate is the work of the freeing of
    the soul!

Open eyes and open heart,

A tongue to speak what must be said

And hands to hold through the terror and
    the pain.

Only those who are themselves becoming free

Can wield this fiery wand.

The rebirth of the soul is an agony and a joy

And only one already reborn

Can assist this painful labour.

How tender and beautiful is the work of the
    freeing of the soul.

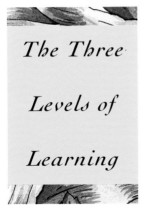

The Three Levels of Learning

One way of understanding why we are the way we are is to look at the past and see how it affected us. How did we turn from hopeful, affectionate, outgoing children to closed-off, despairing or bored adults? I might say it was the way I was brought up or my mother never really cared or my father used to get drunk and beat me or at school they ridiculed me or accused me of cheating or looked down on me.

On the first level of learning, which is the what-they-did-to-me level, this is true and you must tell it to someone, cry about it, write about it or draw pictures of it. Or you can talk aloud or beat a cushion, pretending you are dealing with those who did it to you.

When the first level has been experienced the second level will begin to appear, the level of how-I-coped-with-it. Here you will find the decisions you

made about how to survive in the world, such as: never let anyone close, be quiet and maybe you won't get hurt, be a clown and make them laugh, never let anyone see your real feelings.

Knowing the answers on the second level will not change anything in your life unless the first level has been thoroughly experienced. These decisions we make on the second level have to do with the avoidance of pain. We hold in, hold down and hold back in order to avoid pain for in the depths of our being we fear pain as we fear death. Thus, to move up out of level one you must experience again the pain of those days, feel the loneliness, the stinging blows, the despair of not being understood and you must express it in some way.

Then, and only then, can you begin to work on level two, understanding fully the heartfelt decisions of your childhood. You must understand, not just with your head but in your heart, for the decisions were not made in your head and therefore cannot be unmade in your head.

When level two is complete, level three may appear. This is the level which includes philosophy, religion, poetry, the meaning of life. It is formed of the unknown: unknown darknesses and unknown lights. Here time and space are seen differently from the way they were seen on the first two levels. You are no longer standing in the present looking back at the past and forward into the future; instead, past, present and future exist at one and the same time, the poetic symbol of your life, created by you in the past, sustained by you in the present and projected by you into the future. I call this tense the 'present eternal'.

For example, do you feel as if you are in a trap? Were you trapped last year too? Were you trapped as a teenager? As a child? Have you ever known anything but a trap? Or, are you always second best? Or, do you always miss out? What is your present state? Have you felt like this before? What is the poetic symbol of your life? What would you feel like

9

without that symbol? Free and happy? Frightened? Both? This journey into the unknown, what might it hold? What joys, what terrors?

The trap, or the state of always having a preferred rival, or the missed opportunity, all seem to be fated, to originate in the environment. Shift the viewpoint. How did you make it the way it is? Or, how did you contribute to its being that way? How do you keep it there? What was it for in the beginning? What is it for now?

On this third level, the world is a mirror in which we meet only ourselves, only what we have put there. The creator and the creation are one.

A dream is a private myth;
a myth is a public dream.

Down into the deeps

Down into the deeps of my mind I sink
To find the secret answers
I have hidden from myself over the years.
I am a little afraid of my own dark depths,
But I must search this unknown region
And make it mine.
It is a part of what I am
And I must find its hidden corners
And add them to the continent that is me.
Welcome, dark depths, light up your deeps,
Your creator is entering in.

All the differences

All the differences

And all the dividings

Must be suffered away

When the large work of uniting is going on.

All the sunderings must be put together;

All the misunderstandings must be
    understood;

All that has been unspoken must be spoken;

All the anger suppressed must be released;

All the grief that is left must be wept away;

All the hurt must be said so that the healing
    can happen;

All the fear must be felt so that the strength
    can come;

All the love must be loosed that has been
    hidden away;

Then the large work of uniting will be done.

Creation

A creation always mirrors the artist who created it; it is as small and ugly and false as its creator; it is as wide, as deep, as beautiful as its creator. The larger your soul becomes, the larger your creation will be. A great artist must be able to accept the world the way it is. You must be able to accept what the world contains; you must contain the world. The world must be in you; not you in the world. If you can accept yourself, you can accept the world.

If you are split inside yourself, you meet your unconfronted side in the world in order to become unified within yourself. Light is necessary for growth. If you cannot see the darkness within, it must be illuminated without, so that you can see it, accept it, make it your own and so become enlightened to that degree. The unmanifest must be made manifest. The artist creates himself as well as his creation.

The creator and his creation are two aspects of the same thing, like the body and the soul. Barriers

restrict the creation. The fewer the barriers the greater the creation. A barrier stops things coming in and also stops things going out. It cannot be a one-way fence. You make something and then it makes you.

Creation is a fullness and drives out emptiness. Creation is a flow and drives out stoppedness. Creation is free and unconfined and breaks down fences. Creation is like life: it never runs out because the more you give of it the more you can have and the more you have the more you can give. If your creation ever stops and you think it has run out, be assured, the truth is that you have erected a barrier where there was none before.

If you contain the world you can have anything. If you cannot accept the world or parts of it, you are restricted to that extent and suffer scarcity to that extent.

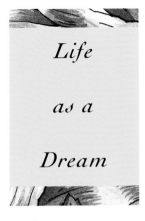

Life

as a

Dream

In a dream we invent everything: situation, landscape, other characters, every happening. We create not only ourselves but also the monster that is chasing us, the mountain we have to climb, the gulf that opens at our feet.

In our waking life, too, something like this is going on. Within the large world which we all inhabit lie the personal worlds, different for each person, created by each person for himself. I create my own world just as surely as I create my dream world. In neither case is the creation a conscious one; it is spun out of the depths of me, often seeming to be the opposite of what my conscious mind wants. In therapy a person often realises and sees vividly how he created a situation of which he has, until then, been the victim.

Are you having a good dream or a night-mare? What sort of life are you dreaming up for yourself?

The soul grows bigger or smaller all the time according to how much you let in or shut out.

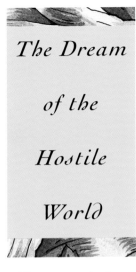

The Dream of the Hostile World

I t is dangerous to become important and noticeable: they cut down the tall poppies. If they see you they'll get you, nail you up, jail, ridicule, destroy you. It's better to stay small and not be noticed, a blameless nonentity.

But

You can only become an enemy of the world if you see the world as hostile to you and as separated from you. That is, if you and the rest of the world are split apart. That is, if you have a split within you, one part against another part. If you are unified within, you will not be in opposition to the world without, for the outer world mirrors the inner world.

If you doubt yourself, you want the world's acceptance. The world cannot accept you if you do not accept yourself. If you have a conflict within, wanting to be large but feeling small, then the world

will act in accordance with the secret smallness and will act to reduce you. If anyone puts you down, makes you look small, they are simply taking the place of the doubting part of you.

The evil in the world is made of the things for which responsibility is not taken; evil is that part of the self which is denied and projected.

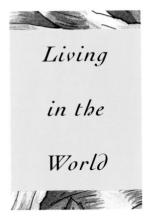

Living

in the

World

Society, like an individual, has its own life, its own level of living and its own pattern. Societies are born, grow strong and lusty, mature, grow old and decay. A society, during its lifetime, may be aggressive, fearful, depressed or apathetic. Society is made up of all the people in it; society's pattern is made up of the combined patterns of all its members. When enough people are full of resentment and anger it may erupt into violence and war. When there is enough anxiety, depression and apathy, a Depression may result. The world pattern is something no one has yet understood. Over the years it has been discussed by philosophers, historians, political theorists, economists, but no theory has yet fully explained it. All we know is that every now and again we, as individuals, are swept up in happenings of historical moment: new technology, war, depression, revolution. At these times there is an

upheaval in the whole society and therefore the individuals in that society have to face a corresponding crisis within their own lives. It is not the crisis itself but how the society or individual meets it that is the important factor. A time of crisis can be a time of growth or a time of defeat, depending on the way we meet it.

Web of the world

In the whole web woven of the being of the
    world

Each of us has a place,

A small corner of the tapestry uniquely ours,

Spun in with our times and those around us.

We weave our own corner into its own shape

And all the tiny shapes become the whole,

And the whole moulds the little shapes

Until all are become part of one another.

No matter how small, all are required;

No matter how unimportant, all are
    necessary;

Each touches the whole and becomes a part
    of it.

Even you, even a small lizard, touches and
    changes

The skirts of the universe.

'If Only'

'I compare what was with what might have been. If I'd been better, I'd have achieved more. If things had been different, I'd be different.

'I compare what is with what might be. If I had someone to love I'd be happy. If I had an easier job I wouldn't feel so pressured.

'I'm never really in the present time. I make the year into a series of mile-posts: kids' birthdays, annual holidays, exams and so on and then I don't have to notice the present. There's all these things to look forward to so that I don't have to notice the emptiness. Life is just something to be got through until you die.

'In the past, things were so bad that if I hadn't hung on to a dream of the future I couldn't have gone on. Now it's a habit I can't break. I'm never in the present.'

We asked this lady, 'What would you do if you only had a year to live?'

She answered, 'I'd just live, but I'd make every minute count.'

We either get better or we get worse; it is not possible to stay the same.

Change

How easy it is for people to change their lives

And yet how hard.

We say — look what the world has done
to me,

It is all their fault.

And we say — if only, if only —

We spend our whole lives making excuses
and blaming others,

Creating and believing the grand illusion

That what happens to us has nothing to
do with us.

How much harder it is

To see how we have very carefully made our
lives

Exactly as they are,

That we are the authors of these messy tales

And we alone can change the story

If we will.

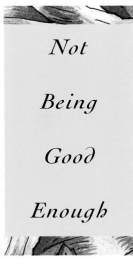

Not Being Good Enough

If you feel you are not good enough, you don't expect to have things. Who are you to expect anything? Possessions, rights, dignity — you are not worthy of these. You must always give more than you get in order to fill the unacceptability gap. At a party you do the washing up or look after the drinks, making up for your lack of worth by being useful.

At work, you have to earn every cent, perhaps work twice as hard to prove to yourself that you are entitled to your pay. If you are very unacceptable you might have to give everything and expect nothing in return. You may feel bitter at the injustice of this. Then you feel bad because you shouldn't be bitter so you do penance by suffering. This makes up

for it in a way, squares accounts, keeps the credit side up.

Enjoyment is the reward of virtue. If you are not good enough, enjoying is cheating and you feel guilty if you do enjoy. You must not have more than enough for bare survival. If you do go out to dinner or a show you say 'it will do me good'. This excuses the enjoyment and turns it from a luxury into a necessity. Like someone who drinks brandy 'for medicinal purposes'.

The feelings of unworthiness must be examined and relinquished; martyrs do not enrich the lives of their companions.

A doormat gets nothing but dirt on its back.

What a burden of fears

What a burden of fears

We all carry.

What a sea of tears

We hide below the surface.

What hidden hates

Eat deep into our hearts.

No wonder our bodies are ill

With these emotions held so still

And pushed into the bones and flesh

So that they will be forgotten.

If only we could undo this mesh,

How free and beautiful we could be.

To hold back from life is to die.

Avoidance

Avoidance may be a big, black pit in your life or it may be only a small, shaky corner. Either way, large or small, it is the danger spot which you walk past with your eyes turned away. The more you turn your eyes away, the bigger and deeper the dark corner grows until at last it can almost fill your life and there is no freedom to move any more.

There is much in life that is painful: feelings of grief, shame, loss, rejection, fear, humiliation, hate, anger, as well as struggle and physical pain. There are many ways of avoiding pain. There is also no way of avoiding pain.

Pain is an inescapable part of living, but people still try to avoid it. You can get drunk or take drugs to cover a bad feeling or a physical pain. You can avoid situations of possible conflict or challenge so that the feelings are not touched. You can avoid emotional involvement for the same reason. You can push the emotion down by sheer willpower.

Try as you might, in the end none of these work. You can't stay drunk or doped all the time; at some stage you must sober up or come down and, when you do, there is the bad feeling waiting for you. If you consistently avoid conflict you become a doormat on which people wipe their feet. If you avoid challenge life becomes boring. If you avoid involvement life becomes meaningless. If you push the emotion down it lodges in the body and makes it sick or prone to accidents.

Avoidance of pain is, ultimately, impossible. If pain is an inescapable part of living then, if life has a basic meaning, pain also has meaning. I have found that whenever I have faced pain instead of avoiding it, spiritual growth has come, bringing knowledge, joy, relief from suffering, increased meaningfulness, more relationship, more creativity; in short, more life.

Today I have run away

Today

I have run away into crowded shops

And jostling thoroughfares

To escape from myself and the misery that is within me.

I have shut myself up behind my face

And moved to where nobody knows me,

Busily buying gifts and running away from my feelings.

Now, on this empty beach,

I can face myself and how I feel,

The paradox of knowing and not knowing,

The agony of loneliness within love,

And the entire contradiction which is me.

Unconsciousness

How can people live as unconsciously as
   they do?

Listening and yet not hearing —

Looking and yet not seeing —

Eating and yet not tasting.

Living behind a wall of separation,

How can they go on being so deaf and
   so dumb

When the whole beautiful world out there

Is beating to come in?

Levels of Living Chart

GENERAL LEVEL	COMMUNICATION	STATE OF RELATIONSHIPS
SELF-ACTUALISING	Spontaneous, free flowing, emotional, direct. Listens and understands.	Deep, long-standing friendships. Appreciative and appreciated. Gets on well with people.
AGGRESSION	Intolerant, argumentative, tends to shout, accuses. Tries to force agreement. Doesn't listen easily.	Fights with people. Controls by threats. Punishes, blames, competes.
RESENTMENT	Covertly hostile. May appear constructive but really undermines. Makes snide comments, gossips, suspects hidden hostility in others. Misinterprets communication. Inhibits the communication of others.	Distrustful, envious, falls out with people. Controls by veiled threats or ridicule. Resents others and gets back at them covertly. Competes covertly. Devious.
ANXIETY	Talks about worries and fears. Wants to know what will happen next. May be a good listener.	Lonely, nervous of people. Wants help, protection and reassurance. Protective of others.
DEPRESSION	Pessimistic. Talks mainly about their own miseries or the misfortunes of others. May cry easily. Listen mainly to things that relate to themselves.	Withdrawn and miserable. Feels alone.
APATHY	Doesn't bother to talk. Doesn't bother to listen.	None. Can't make the effort. May control others by being helpless and/or pathetic.

SELF IMAGE	NEEDS	SEXUAL RELATIONS	ATTITUDE TO LIFE
Likes and accepts self. Neither superior nor inferior.	Freedom to create and grow.	Mutually loving and fulfilling, stable.	Optimistic, involved, flexible, emotional. Pursues own interests with enthusiasm and creativity.
Superior and right.	Acceptance and belonging.	Dominating, inconsiderate.	Ambitious. Oppressive. Prejudiced.
Superior, right, clever and unappreciated. Presents social front of pleasantness.	Recognition.	Covertly punishes. Makes inferior.	Secretive, ambitious, authoritarian and prejudiced. Dissatisfied.
Inferior, weak, anxious, tense. Very conscious of own imperfections. May present confident front.	Safety.	Anxious.	Fearful. Accepts authority. May try to be faultless.
Worthless, guilty, weak, suffering, regretful. Victim of circumstance. May present cheerful front.	Hope.	Passive.	Pessimistic. Hopeless. Wants someone else to take charge.
Helpless victim.	Comfort.	No interest.	Doesn't care. Self-absorbed. Accepts authority.

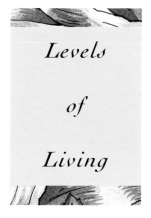

Levels of Living

The Levels of Living chart is not a rigid system, an infallible guide to human nature, but it is a good way to begin looking at people. With its help it is possible to make some sense of the vast web of interlocking relationships we see around us every day.

The first column, General Level, is a list of emotional states. Some people go through a wide range of feelings from day to day; others are chronically fixed in one state of mind only, so that no matter what the circumstances they always complain or no matter what you say they always react angrily. The General Level indicates the feeling the person experiences most of the time.

The order in which they are listed is based on how much or how little the person feels causative about his life. That is, on the lowest level, Apathy, he feels completely the effect of everything and sees himself as a victim of circumstance. On the highest level, Self-actualising, he sees himself as in charge of his life, as responsible for whatever is wrong with it and as capable of changing what he does not like.

A person's level of living also affects her health. Those on the level of apathy are lacking in energy and tend to suffer from some chronic illness, while on self-actualising they are energetic and generally healthy. As a person slips down into the lower levels she becomes increasingly susceptible to infection, illness, accidents and drug dependence. As she improves, she no longer needs alcohol or drugs to make her feel better. She is more energetic and less inclined to suffer from infection, illness or accidents.

The ratio of self-as-cause and self-as-victim varies between these two poles. In detail, the levels are as follows:

1. APATHY

On this level, the person sees himself as a victim of circumstance and as helpless to do anything about it. He does not initiate things; they happen to him. He says, 'I've given up'. The Australian poet, Henry Lawson, describes this state in his poem, 'Past Carin''.

I've grown to be past carin',
Past worryin' and wearin';
I've pulled three through and buried two
Since then and I'm past carin'.

The apathetic person is often chronically ill and lacking in energy. The only way he can relate to others is by receiving their help, for he is so overwhelmed by his own condition that he has no interest or caring left for others. Whatever help is offered or given to him will not basically change anything, because he would rather blame circumstances than be recalled to the struggle of life and take the risk of failing yet again. All he wants is to be comfortable.

2. DEPRESSION

There are degrees of depression from mild to very deep, but the general symptoms are very similar. They can be summed up by the words of a friend. He walked into the house, sat down, put his head in his hands and said slowly: 'Doom! Doom! Doom!'

Depressed people have little or no pleasure in their lives. They feel unworthy and never good enough no matter how much they try, so that their days are a struggle that never ends. They feel powerless and there is no meaning in their lives. As one client said: 'I'm just filling up my time until I die.'

Some will present a cheerful front to the world to hide their inner desperation, so that their families and friends are shocked if they finally have a breakdown or commit suicide. They often have an internal voice which chatters incessantly in their heads telling them what a failure they are.

Fortunately, for many depressed people,

their discomfort and misery will bring them to seek help; they need to find an understanding therapist who will help them work through their painful and often suppressed memories and emotions which they carry like a black burden. Then they can begin their journey into the light and into a happier and more satisfying life.

3. ANXIETY

What will happen if I make a mess of this job, if my lover leaves me, if the business fails, if my child gets sick? What did they think of me in class yesterday? If only I hadn't said or done this or that. Have I made the right decision in buying now?

These are the preoccupations of the person in chronic anxiety. He is always in the past or the future, never in the present. He is everlastingly doubting himself and goes to great lengths to try and be without fault. Since it is

humanly impossible to be faultless he spends a
lot of time in self-recrimination. He continually
seeks reassurance from others but even when
they assure him he did well he never feels good
enough. On the other hand he is only too ready
to believe anything critical that is said about
him because it secretly confirms his worst
suspicions.

He is often a reliable friend because, knowing how terrible it is to feel worried and
unsafe, he tends to protect and help others. In
his deep need to be acceptable he may cover
up his self-doubt and present a confident front.
He often seeks help to improve but never feels
he is progressing fast enough.

The breaking of this level begins when the
person realises he does not have to be faultless
in order to be good enough, that he does not
have to come top, to work long hours or to
endlessly put others first in order to be
acceptable and that he too has rights.

4. RESENTMENT

There are very many people in our society on this level. Resentment is a state midway between fear and anger and its hallmark is secrecy. The person has a great deal of hostility inside but hides it behind a charming manner so that it is hard to believe that there is any hostile intent. He puts others down in a joking way or makes critical remarks in order to 'help' them. He also hides his fear, because he wants to appear superior.

People everywhere tend to think others are like themselves and so the resentment level person thinks everyone has hidden hostility. This is another reason for his secrecy. If you trust no one, you will hide yourself from everyone. At the same time as he is hiding he secretly craves recognition. He feels he is really better than others, but no one appreciates it. He has 'potential' and thinks this should be recognised, but is afraid to develop any talent in case others put him down.

The resentful person has a relationship pattern of becoming 'best friends' with someone only to 'fall out' with them later. The reason for this is that sooner or later some little thing happens which annoys or upsets him but he does not clear the air by telling his friend. Instead, he hides it and the next time something happens he adds that to it until soon there is so much secret resentment that the friendship (or marriage) comes to an end.

If you are in a personal or work relationship with a resentful person and do not recognise what he is up to, you may sink into anxiety and confusion, because he is constantly giving you hostile messages disguised as friendly ones. If you do realise what is going on, you may feel frustrated and powerless because he has you in a 'no win' position. Whatever you say or do is

wrong. The best way to deal with such a person is to confront him openly with what he is saying covertly and to refuse to be involved in his secrets. That is, you do not play his game, you expose it.

If someone in resentment is to raise his level he must be prepared to give up his secrets, to express his fear and anger openly and honestly, to confess his mean thoughts, to lay himself open to others. Only then will he be freed from the chains that bind him, that stop him developing his potential, that keep him small. Freedom and joy cannot come to a person whose life is hedged about with secrets.

5. AGGRESSION

The people in a chronic state of aggression have anger on the surface and fear underneath. They tend to meet opposition wherever they go and if the opposition is not there in the beginning, their antagonism soon produces it. They are intolerant, argumentative and dogmatic. They know they are right and will not waste their time listening to others. If anyone thinks differently from themselves, then that person is wrong. They are usually married to a little washed-out victim of a person over whom they tyrannise. They do not usually seek help because they know better than anyone else. Also, because they are so aggressive they generally get their own way. They are more likely to send their wives, husbands or children off to be cured than go themselves.

6. SELF-ACTUALISING

This is the only really healthy level. Everywhere below this is what is usually called 'normal neurotic'. The state of being self-actualising simply means that the person is in the process of actualising his potential. He is not 'self-actualised', for such a state does not, as far as I know, exist. There is no point where growth ceases, no point of arrived perfection.

As one grows and develops, so more potential comes into view and as you 'actualise' each bit you have to plough your way through the things that have blocked off that bit in the past. At times you run the gamut of almost every emotion there is but you do not sink chronically into the lower levels. Since you know you are the cause of the way you are, you soon discover the basis of the 'down' mood and take steps to get through it.

Because people on this level see themselves as causative, they are not afraid of becoming the effect of others. Thus, having but little fear, their energies flow freely and, since sickness is the result of blocked energy, they are usually healthy as well as energetic. They enjoy encouraging others, creating, bringing clarity out of confusion, order out of chaos. They are optimistic about life and people and have honest and mutually satisfying relationships with others.

All

Levels

It should be remembered that the chart must be read flexibly. For example, a person may be in anxiety at work and aggressive at home or vice versa. Nor does someone pass rigidly through each level as he improves. The important thing to remember is that one's level can be changed. You are not born a depressed type or an anxious type or an aggressive type. Anyone who is prepared to do the necessary work on him/herself can develop into a psychologically healthy, creative, self-actualising individual.

At last I am tapping

At last I am tapping again

The deep wild river hidden below,

Shut away but roaring in my ears.

Who knows what divine madness

Will come from such freeing

And what fear and rough crossing,

But once launched on these magic waters

There is no safe return to dry land again.

Energy

If you stop an energy flow you get a tight lump of squashed energy which will probably manifest as a headache, a stomach upset, tension, a cold, any of the minor ailments we all suffer from. This is a destructive way of using the energy.

If you outflow energy you do not use it up, because it is not a fixed quantity. It is more like electricity: if you flow it out, more must flow in. The more you allow your energy to flow, the more there is and hence the more energy you have coming in through you.

A bore is someone who has no interest in anything (except perhaps himself). Because he is not interested he is not interesting. Nothing flows out and nothing flows in. If you are bored you are boring.

Ability is dependent on energy flow. Ability may be actualised and flowing or it may be potential. Either way it is not a fixed quantity. That is, as more ability becomes manifest, it does not leave a smaller residue

of potential. As it is with energy, so it is with ability. The more you get the potential into use and actualise it the more potential there is left, because it is a continuous flow, a bottomless abyss fountaining up more and more potential, the more it is used. Thus there is no ceiling on one's ability for there is always more available. The only requirement is the persistence to go on bringing out what is there.

Conversely, if you begin to shut off and stop using what is there, the potential ability lessens. The more shut off you get, the more restricted is the flow and so the quality of your life and of everything you do deteriorates.

Look out at things and people, reach out to them, flow out to them, and life will flow into you in ever-increasing abundance.

Suffering

The story is told that when Persephone was imprisoned in the Underworld her mother, Demeter, sought her for many a weary day. In the course of her wanderings she took shelter with a young couple and was employed by them to care for their child.

Demeter grew fond of this child and decided to make him immortal. In order to accomplish this she had to put him each night into the fire so that his mortality would be burned away. However, one night the parents discovered her laying the child in the fire and in terror chased her from the house. Thus the child never achieved the status which was intended: the status of a god.

Suffering is the crucible through which life passes in order to purify itself. It is not enough to lie still and suffer; it does not suffice to switch off and render ourselves insensitive. We must fight through it with awareness, sensitivity, honesty and a full-blooded

determination to keep our humanity. Only then will our mortality be burned away and the spirit find its truth.

Cynicism is a protection against vulnerability.

Strength

Inside,

I am making myself strong.

I am weaving bands of steel

To bind my soul.

I am knitting stitches of suffering

Into my hands

To make them strong.

I am strengthening my mind

With the warp and weft

Of weariness and endurance.

I am binding my faith

With the bonds of psalms and songs

Of all who have suffered.

In time,

I will be tempered like fine steel

To bend, but not to break.

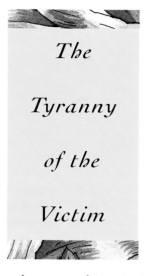

The Tyranny of the Victim

There are different degrees of victimhood. All of us, in varying degrees, are victims; that is, all of us, in some areas of our lives, see ourselves as the effect of things rather than as the cause of things. Some people are only mild victims whereas others are big victims. The victim game is widespread, if not universal. Husbands are the victims of wives and wives are the victims of husbands; children are the victims of parents and parents are the victims of children; teachers are the victims of students and students are the victims of teachers and so on.

Where there is a victim there is also a tyrant and sometimes it is difficult to tell who is victimising who. For example, it is a strange paradox that the biggest victims are also the biggest tyrants. Whether the victim says it in words or whether he only implies it, his message is, 'You must help me because I am helpless. If I were strong and capable like you I wouldn't ask. It's not my fault I'm weak/frightened/poor/tired/sick/incapable/unloved/etc.' The person who gets trapped in this situation, not the one who consciously decides to help and feels good about it, but the one who actually feels guilty for being strong/secure/loved/capable/well/energetic/etc., must then put all his strength into serving the weak. He is at the beck and call of the victim.

For example, the victim has been turned out of his flat and has nowhere to live? Of course he can stay and sleep in the living room. It would be heartless to refuse. He can't pay for his food at present because he has no money? Of course he can share mine. It means I have to work overtime or go without the sound system I was saving up for but after all, that

doesn't really matter — I mean, he's got to eat, hasn't he? His gear makes a bit of a mess in the living room and we can't have visitors any more, but it will only be for a little while. I really think he should have asked about bringing his girlfriend to stay as well, but I can see the difficulty he was in. After all, she has no money either, and I suppose it will only be for another month or two . . . And so on and on until the victim is tyrannising over the whole household.

Once the victim's basic premise is accepted the rest follows. The basic premise rests on the claim that the victim is not responsible for his situation and can therefore do nothing to change it. So long as you go along with this by doing for him what he cannot do for himself you are agreeing that he cannot do it. You are absolving him from being responsible for himself. This reinforces his neurotic pattern. He need never grow strong while he can rely on the strength of others.

Now for the lesser victim. She rings you up and asks you to go out with her on Saturday night. You don't want to go; she is always complaining about her situation and you are sick of hearing about it. However, the un-spoken message that comes across in her tone of voice and manner of asking is, 'Don't you reject me; I have so few friends.' So you say, 'Thank you, I'd love to come.' The evening is just as you knew it would be; she moans all the time and you can't get a word in edgewise. You can't tell her to shut up because she'd be so hurt. Once again, here is the same paradox of the strength of the weak and the weakness of the strong. She has organised you on an outing you didn't want; she has persecuted you all evening with her talk; she has rendered you powerless to object and yet she is supposed to be the one who is weak and you are supposed to be the strong one.

Of course you may decide not to accept the invitation but to make an excuse instead, so

that when she asks, you say, 'I'd love to go but I'm much too busy this week.' It may even be partly true, but if some exciting friend rang and asked you out you'd manage to go somehow. You have avoided her demands by pretending to be a victim yourself. Your unspoken message to her then becomes something like, 'It's all very well for you; you can go out and enjoy yourself but I can't; I have to stay home and work.' Out-victiming the victim like this is the only legitimate way of refusing her demands because it is the only refusal that leaves her victim game intact. Should you simply say, 'No, I don't want to go', without making any excuses, this denies her right to make demands on you. It is very difficult for most people to say no, to assert their own rights rather than to submit to the demands of others, and yet this is the only way to break the neurotic bind you are in. Victims have an uncanny way of making others feel guilty and people often prefer to give in to the victim's demands rather than feel mean.

The essential thing in any discussion on victims is to consider how much we are playing victims ourselves. It is much easier to see what others are doing than to see our part in it, and if we concentrate on seeing only how other people are to blame there will be no improvement. Therefore we should notice, firstly, what demands we make on others, our families, our close friends. Have we any right to make these demands? If we do have special rights, are these based on an aspect of weakness or victimhood in ourselves? Do people have to be nice to me because I have had a hard time? Because I am poor? Because I am valiantly struggling against terrible odds? And so on.

Secondly, to be taken in by a victim (thereby becoming his victim) you have to be something of a victim yourself. If you believe that there is

something in someone else's life for which he is not responsible, then there is also something in your life for which you feel you are not responsible. For example, you say you cannot speak out because the other person is too weak to take it. That is, you are not responsible for your silence; he is. Probably the real reason is that you are afraid to cope with his response. His weakness is your excuse for your weakness. It is a conspiracy; weakness encourages weakness. If a person who is not playing victims asks you to do something you will probably find it easy to refuse because the request will be put in a way that allows for a refusal. The person is strong enough to take a refusal and so you have the choice. That is, strength permits strength.

Victimhood is the basis of much of our suffering. A victim is clustered around with excuses like a ship with barnacles. If you notice yourself making an excuse (and who of us doesn't make them?) either to yourself or to others, you may rest assured that somewhere you are being a victim. If you see yourself as a victim in some particular area, then that is the area in which you are rendering yourself powerless. Once you accept the fact that you are creating your own life every moment of every day, then you can begin to untie the chains and to create it differently.

A trained slave will tolerate anything; a spoilt child nothing. There must be a balance.

Freedom

A person is free when she is not operating within a pattern. The philosopher, William James, defined freedom as, 'a certain looseness in the conjunction of things'. This looseness is just what is missing in any basic life pattern, for a pattern is a tight and perfect construction in which everything locks together absolutely.

There is a certain security in having a pattern. Without one, *anything* can happen; with one, only those things within the pattern can happen; that is, only things which have happened before. When you move into the environment of a person with a very strong pattern he locks you straight into the pattern. It is like stepping into a part in a play written by someone else. Whatever you say or do is misinterpreted so that it fits into the person's expectations. He doesn't see *you*; he sees whatever he expects to see according to his pattern.

When a pattern goes there is a feeling of not knowing anything. You face the world as if for the first time, having no standard to measure it by, no system to explain it, no fence to hold it off. Freedom can be very frightening.

The world is a mirror; wherever you go you meet only yourself.

The Unconscious

There is a small amount of consciousness and a large amount of unconsciousness. It is as if consciousness is a later development in evolution. People are afraid of the unconscious. It is so large and formless that no one knows the extent of it. It is of great antiquity and mostly unknown. Who would not be afraid? It seems to be made of raw soul-stuff or the raw material of the universe. Perhaps it is infinite, part of the chaos that was before creation.

It is said, 'Now the earth was unformed and void and darkness was upon the face of the deep . . . ' This is how I see the unconscious: deep, covered in darkness and formless, but full of potential creation.

People in their fear build walls against it. Some have such thick ones they deny its existence, repress all feelings, praise the rational above all else and, with their eyes blindfolded, walk a tightrope over the abyss. These must learn to listen to their hearts, to feel the fragile fingertips of the emotions they have almost forgotten, to find again the wonder and the fear of their dreams, to reclaim the whole riches of the inner world.

Others have such a thin line between themselves and the unconscious that they slip all too easily into the darkness and, leaving consciousness behind, fall into madness. These must put all their energies into being aware of the physical world around them — look at the streets, the people, the trees, the sky; touch fences, grass, walls, water; feel the hot sun, the cold wind, the smoothness of polished wood, the roughness of brick and stone; smell flowers and petrol fumes and dust and rain after drought. They must leave behind their endless wanderings in the maze of the mind and step into the bright freedom of reality.

The balance between the inner and the outer worlds must be corrected. If the inner is

denied, the springs of life are blocked off and the soul becomes narrow, rigid and dry. If the outer is denied, one is swept by raging winds of emotion which one is powerless to control. The task is to be firmly rooted in the physical world and to explore the border country between the worlds. We must take our consciousness and walk gently into the subconscious, pushing back the borders of the unknown. As explorers have done with the far lands of the world, so we must do with the world of the mind, not only for understanding and improvement but for safety as well. The unconscious, suppressed for a lifetime, can erupt violently; brought into partnership with the conscious mind, it can give strength, beauty, creativity, love. Step by step we must light up the edge of the darkness.

Some of this work can be done alone; for much we need a companion and guide. If she has never walked in such lands herself, nor learnt to live fully, she cannot guide another through them or teach another to live fully. Choose your guide with care.

I have not understood

I have not understood what has been
  happening within me

These past two months.

Roaring oceans of grief have assailed me.

My world has fallen into tatters in my
  hands.

My past has risen like a dragon and
  swallowed me up,

Invading my present and twisting it up like
  crumpled paper.

I think I have been loosening my bonds,

Casting off from the past,

And out of what seemed to be terrible
  weakness,

Creating a new and magnificent strength.

Patterns

Almost everyone has a basic pattern for survival. We do not live life spontaneously, responding to each new situation as it arises. Instead, we live by habit; the old tried and tested response is the one we feel safest with. Usually a pattern of response is set up in childhood and we live the rest of our lives according to ways of coping we worked out when we were very young.

For example, a child is sent to school. He is a sensitive person whose mind seems to work differently from the other children's. He is laughed at or rejected or attacked for his difference. This is very painful for him. How is he to deal with the situation?

This is a problem common to many people, but each person responds in his or her own way. William suppressed his difference and thereby lost a very important part of himself: his creativity, his uniqueness, the very springs of his being. John became hard and

cold and cut off his feelings altogether. Marie grew very shy and withdrawn, speaking only when spoken to, keeping her thoughts to herself, hiding in the back seats and becoming as invisible as possible. Sebastian became the school clown, so that when he said something people could never tell whether he was joking or not. This kept them at a safe distance and if they laughed, instead of feeling a fool, he knew he was just playing the fool. Jane avoided the pain of rejection by having frequent bilious attacks so that often she did not have to go to school at all.

Each of these people developed patterns, or habits of coping, out of a healthy desire to survive but each paid the price in the end, stepping down from a high level of full life and energy into something much less; they gained life by lessening life.

William came to therapy because he felt he was wishy-washy, unsatisfactory as a person, as a husband and as a father. John wanted to have close relationships but could not get in touch with his feelings. Marie's problem was that people did not notice her and she was continually passed over for promotion. Sebastian complained that people didn't take him seriously. Jane was ill whenever she tried to go anywhere where she would be part of a group.

It is not what happens to us that sets the pattern of our lives but the way we respond to what happens.

Once set up, patterns are very tenacious because they are made of the person's life-force. She does not see herself as separate from the pattern. She thinks that this way of being is her way of being; it is her identity. If you attack a person's basic pattern directly she feels it as a direct attack on herself. Try helping to relieve the burden from someone who is valiantly struggling on alone against over-

whelming odds. She won't let you. Her identity is defined as the lone and valiant struggler. Without the struggle, what would there be to admire? Usually it is only when the pattern will not work any more that the person is prepared to try and get rid of it and even then it takes great courage and persistence to do so. Until this time comes, any helpful suggestions from you will invariably be met by, 'Yes, but if I do that . . . ' or 'Yes, that's a good idea, but . . . ' If someone keeps saying, 'Yes, but . . . ' you will know that you are up against a pattern and may as well give up suggesting things.

The reason it is so difficult to break a pattern is that it was originally set up for survival; that is, it was made when the situation was so bad that the person feared he would not survive it. This means that to break a pattern he must face the fear of death.

When the pattern begins to break, the feelings that created the need for the pattern will turn on, and the person will feel that if he persists in his attempt to break the pattern he will die or go mad. In fact, the opposite is true. If the pattern is broken the person will live and go sane, really sane; that is, fully alive, creative and free.

The task is to disentangle the soul.

Patterns

in

Partners

People become deeply involved with those whose patterns match theirs. For instance, Mike's pattern is one of loss. He is careful never to get so involved with someone that if he lost them he could not cope. He expects to lose and builds his behaviour around this expectation. Helen's pattern is one of rejection. She is afraid of having someone slam the door in her face. In order to avoid this she is careful never to force herself on anyone or make any demands or complain about anything. 'If they don't like me, I'll go away,' she says. She expects to get rejected and builds her behaviour around this expectation.

Mike and Helen fall in love. 'Don't ever leave me,' he murmurs tenderly. 'Promise to love me always,' she replies passionately. And we hope they will live happily ever after. However, there are the patterns lurking underneath.

One day Helen comes home later than expected. Mike seems a little cool. 'What's the matter?' asks Helen. 'Nothing; I'm just a bit worried about this job that we're starting on Tuesday.' She accepts his answer and although all that evening he seems a little distant she does not push herself on him when he has more important things to think about.

In a very small way the patterns have begun operating. On a completely unconscious level, Mike has begun holding Helen off against the inevitable day of loss. Helen has begun, also without realising it, to avoid rejection by not making demands. Uninspected, the patterned behaviour builds up, with Helen feeling more and more rejected, but never saying so, while Mike feels more and more that he is losing her and so holds her off further. In the end Helen feels so rejected that she rushes off and has an affair with someone else, just to prove that *someone* wants her. When Mike gets extremely agitated and upset she is amazed. 'Why

shouldn't I?' she asks. 'You don't care about me any more.' 'How could you do this to me?' he cries.

At this stage the relationship could be patched up again but unless the pattern is unravelled it will be only a matter of time before it happens all over again and ends in Mike and Helen going off in opposite directions, both swearing never to get in another situation like that. And how will they make sure they don't? Mike will hold people off even more because he is now still more afraid of loss and Helen will be even more careful not to expose herself to rejection. We can guess what will happen with their next partners.

What is the way out of these knotted bonds? You must have communication, awareness, total honesty, willing vulnerability. If all these are present the pattern need never escalate. At the first sign of something strange happening in the relationship you must talk about it. Your awareness of what is going on must be increased. Your own feelings must be conveyed with total honesty, even if it sounds silly. This means you lay yourself wide open to whatever your partner may say. If the reply upsets you this too must be explored. It often happens that the very thing you dare not say is the thing that is right at the heart of the matter.

For instance, that first night when Helen came home late, she secretly wondered if Mike was upset because of her lateness but she did not ask him for fear he would blame her and say hurtful things and besides, why would anyone, even Mike, want *her*? Mike himself really knew it was Helen's being late that had upset him but he would sound silly and childish if he said so and anyway it probably *was* the job that was really worrying him. So, although somewhere both knew what was going on, neither would speak.

It is often just these small things that seem

too petty to mention that sow the seeds for real trouble later. This is because, although small in themselves, they represent something much bigger, a lifetime's pattern. For a relationship to succeed, both partners must be fully committed to working through whatever turns up, with complete honesty about themselves. The bonus is that not only will the relationship be ever-growing and never boring, but the individuals concerned will break their patterns and so break out of their smallness into more strength, energy, warmth and creativity.

If you do not want to understand a person,
tie a label on him.

How the past ties our hands

How the past ties our hands and ties our
   minds

Into tight closed patterns.

How much are our whole lives

Grooved into narrow moulds by the past;

Our emotions closed into little, shut
   cupboards

And the keys lost;

Our failures tied round our necks

Like old tins on a string

Rattling at all we do;

Our fears sitting on our shoulders like heavy
   packs

No matter how we run.

O let me break my chains!

Let my burdens go!

Let me find the key and be free!

Forgetting

Where is the past? Has it vanished altogether? Is it still present because of memories? If we do not remember it as it really was, does this change it? If we forget it, is it gone? Or does it exist forever on some timeless plane? No one knows the answers but we all find ways to deal with the past. Some of these are creative, some destructive.

The commonest way is to try and forget the unpleasant things that happened. As one lady, a refugee from Hitler, said to me, 'What is the good to look to the shadows?' Naturally we try to avoid pain and, unless something forces us to face it, we do try to forget.

What is forgetting? Forgetting is making something conscious into something unconscious. If we are struggling to grow into ever greater awareness, wholeness, sensitivity, this is a backward step and at some stage will have to be reversed for growth to take place. A decrease of consciousness means a decrease in ability, in potential, in health, in intelligence, in the power to enjoy, in life itself. For some the memories may be so bad that they are glad to pay the price. To them we cannot speak. To those who are of two minds about it we say the greater the pain, the more the need to face it and the greater the inrush of life when it is done. From the facing of suffering, great wisdom can come. Why pay the price and not get the goods?

Consciousness is catching.

Tears of all the world

Why am I so choked with grief, so full of
 tears?

I have had sadness enough these last few
 years;

It is surely done and past.

But inside I have an ocean of grief

Welling up from some deep depths

Below my memory,

Weighing me down with the accumulated
 tears of centuries.

I find it hard enough to cope with my own
 grief,

But without help

I could drown in the tears of the whole
 world.

Eyes

I have a pair of ugly eyes which I often use,

And out of them the sights that I see

Are hard and ugly and hateful and grey.

I see fear and I see lies —

I see killing and I see abuse —

I see blaming and I see misuse —

There is no mistaking the misery that I see.

I have a pair of beautiful eyes which I like
to use,

And out of them the sights that I see

Are beautiful and lovely and true.

I see love and babies growing —

I see friendship and oceans flowing —

I see giving and I see creating —

And of the beauty of all there is no
mistaking.

Feast your eyes

Feast your eyes on the tops of the trees,

Drink in the dark greenness of the tall gums,

Walk on the firm ground with bare feet

*And absorb the stuff of the earth into your
     bare soles.*

Take branches into your hands,

Feel the leaves with your face

And take in the inner growing of the tree.

Lie close on the leaves of grass

And let them caress your body.

Take the hot sun into your soul

And let the whole sky sweep into your mind.

Give yourself back to the living earth

And the earth will give itself to you

In unmeasured and unbounded pleasure.

The Future

Some people see the future as something that will eventually roll along to them, just like a train pulling into a station. They wait hopefully for this train to bring them what they wish for: someone to love, a pleasant place to live, freedom from worry and so on. It is a kind of psychological cargo cult.

But the future is not like this. Just as our present is the result of our past, so our future will be the result of our present. Every minute of every day we are weaving the threads that will make the cloth of the future.

Most often we will go on weaving the future in the same pattern we have woven the past. We must look at the cloth we have now and if it is not pleasing we must see how we have woven it and start changing the pattern.

Every tiny decision we make — into the world or

away from it, towards creativity or towards failure, decisions to face truth, decisions to avoid — all these are tiny threads of the whole pattern. None must be neglected, not the smallest, or the pattern will begin to follow that stray thread until it controls the whole. It is no use saying, 'I will avoid this now but in years to come, when I am stronger, I will face it'; what you do now you will do later. We must weave always, consistently, the pattern we want or we will not have the future we wish for.

Reading List

This is a list of classic texts which are as fresh and important today as when they were first published.

Dyer, Wayne: *Your Erroneous Zones*. Good for all the usual problems people have: seeking approval, poor self-image, negative outlook on life, guilt etc.

Frankl, Viktor: *Man's Search for Meaning*. A psychiatrist who survived concentration camp and found that people need to feel their lives have a meaning.

Jung, Carl Gustav: *Memories, Dreams and Reflections*. Autobiography: a fascinating portrait of a fascinating man. Jung's basic discoveries about the mind.

Maslow, Abraham: Any of his many books.

May, Rollo: *The Art of Counselling*.

Meares, Dr Ainsley: *Relief Without Drugs*.

Montague, Dr Ashley: *Touching*. On the importance of touching for psychological health.

Rogers, Carl: *On Becoming a Person.*

Sheehy, Gail: *Passages.* Describes the change points in people's lives at each decade and the problems that must be faced at these times in order to move smoothly into the next phase of living.

Simonton, O.C., S. Mathews Simonton, and J.L. Creighton: *Getting Well Again.* This book deals with a new psychological approach for people with cancer. These methods may be applied to many other illnesses.

Since *Below the Surface* was first published in 1982, so many, many books have been written on men and women, divorce, bereavement, incest, domestic violence, anxiety, depression, anorexia, children of alcoholic parents, conflict resolution, etc., etc., that it is impossible to list them here. Some are good and some are not. Find the ones that are simple and speak to you.

BY ANNE SPENCER PARRY

The Land Behind the World, 1976
The Lost Souls of the Twilight, 1977
The Crown of Darkness, 1979
The Crown of Light, 1980
Below the Surface, Reflections on Life and Living, co-author
with Marjorie Pizer, 1982
Zaddik and the Seafarers, 1983
Beyond the Outlandish Mountains, 1984

BY MARJORIE PIZER

Thou and I, Poems, 1967
To Life, Poems, 1969
Tides Flow, Poems, 1972
Seasons of Love, Poems, 1975
Full Summer, Poems, 1977
Gifts and Remembrances, Poems, 1979
To You, The Living, Poems of Bereavement and Loss, 1981,
1991, 1992
The Sixtieth Spring, Poems, 1982
Below the Surface, Reflections on Life and Living, co-author
with Anne Spencer Parry, 1982
Selected Poems, 1963–1983, 1984
The Poems of Lesbia Harford, co-editor with
Drusilla Modjeska, 1985
Equinox, Poems, 1987
Fire in the Heart, Poems, 1990
Journeys, Poems, 1992

An Angus & Robertson Publication

Angus&Robertson, an imprint of
HarperCollins*Publishers*
25 Ryde Road, Pymble, Sydney, NSW 2073, Australia
31 View Road, Glenfield, Auckland 10, New Zealand
77-85 Fulham Palace Road, London W6 8JB, United Kingdom
10 East 53rd Street, New York NY 10022, USA

National Library of Australia
Cataloguing-in-Publication data:

Parry, Anne Spencer, 1931-
Below the surface.

New ed.
ISBN 0 207 18043 1.

1. Self-realisation. I. Pizer, Marjorie, 1920- .II. Title.

158.1

Printed in Hong Kong

5 4 3 2 1
98 97 96 95 94